GW00939394

Who is this booklet

This booklet is for Sixth Form students trying to juggle homework, coursework, revision and life!

How can it help?

This booklet contains practical tips that:

✓ help you to keep on top of your workload
✓ help you to get more from your study time
✓ help you to study more effectively

What's in it?

WARNING!
DO NOT READ THIS BOOKLET
FROM START TO FINISH.
Dip into it when you need to!

Using this booklet

Do

✓ Flick through the booklet to see what each of the sections is about and which sections grab your attention.

✓ Try out the tips that appeal to you and don't be afraid to change them to suit you.

✓ Add any new ideas you like to the methods you already have for studying and managing your time.

✓ Keep the booklet in a handy place and dip into it from time to time to give you a boost.

✓ Make notes and highlight ideas you like as you go along.

✓ Start by thinking about the areas of studying and managing your time that you would like some help with.

Don't

✗ Stop using any of your own methods if they have worked for you in the past.

✗ Try to implement all the ideas at once.

✗ Read the booklet through from start to finish.

Increasing
MOTIVATION

Motivation is one of the strongest influences on a student's performance. Lose your motivation and you risk losing the plot completely!

Have high expectations

The most valuable asset you can have is a positive attitude.

If you have high expectations of yourself and believe that you will succeed, you are more likely to reach your potential. Fear of failure is like an invisible barrier which stops you from achieving your potential. If you are the sort of person who is always running yourself down and telling yourself how badly you are going to do, STOP RIGHT NOW!

Find your 'personal benefit'

Why are you studying the courses you have chosen? Where exactly are they leading you? If you can answer these two simple questions then you probably have already found your 'personal benefit'.

Your own 'personal benefit' might be:
- ✓ enjoying the subjects you are studying
- ✓ going to university

✓ doing an apprenticeship
✓ a career you wish to pursue
✓ a satisfying job
✓ a dream lifestyle you want
✓ earning lots of money

One idea you could try is to write your 'personal benefit' on a piece of paper and stick it up at the place where you do most of your studying as a reminder.

Set goals for your courses

Your goals are more specific than a general 'personal benefit' and can be described in terms of the final grades you get at the end of the A level/BTEC courses you are studying. It helps a great deal if you write down the grades you are hoping to achieve and remind yourself of these goals from time to time.

Take a real interest in your courses

If you are interested in a subject it is more likely that you will put in the hours of study required. When you are studying a subject which you find boring, every minute spent studying can seem like an hour and every hour like a day!

You can create interest by asking yourself why the courses you are studying matter. Try to link what you're learning to your own life and the world you live in. Creating an initial spark of interest is usually enough to get the ball rolling.

Get regular feedback

Feedback is essential for any student wanting to make improvements. The grades your teacher gives you for set work and the results you get for tests are an important source of feedback. However, results on their own give very little information about what aspects of your studies you should be working on.

Try to get into the habit of asking your teacher to make full comments about your work. Most teachers are very thorough in what they write on homework and assignments but others aren't and need to be encouraged to do so. If you want spoken feedback, ask your teacher when would be convenient to see them, rather than expecting it to be done during normal lesson times.

When you are being given written or spoken feedback the first step is to make sure you understand the comments being made. Try not to jump to conclusions and be defensive but really listen to the feedback and decide whether it is valid or not. Then decide what action you will take in the future in response to the feedback.

Be competitive

Competition can be a great motivator for some people. You can compete with yourself by keeping a page in the front of each of your main folders where you record all the grades you get for homework and assignments and tests throughout the course. This will help you track your progress and will also highlight topics which you find difficult.

You can compete with others in your class or group by working to improve your position in the class, or by competing directly with a particular person who normally achieves slightly better results than you do. It's probably best that you don't tell the other person that you're doing this!

Celebrate success!

Celebrating is essential when you have completed a major task or when a module/unit comes to an end.

Decide before you begin a project how you'll celebrate when you've finished it. Are you going to go somewhere special, do something you really enjoy or give yourself a day off from your studies?

Arranging to do something with friends who are following the same course means you can all look forward to celebrating together!

2

Time Management BASICS

> Time management is not about being busy or planning your life away. Time management is about getting what you want out of your time!

Suits you

It is important to develop effective habits for organising your time. However, the approach you take to managing your time must take account of the kind of person you are and your circumstances.

Once you've got a good approach to managing your time up and running, work to improve it and adapt it as your circumstances change.

Be clear about what's involved

Find out at the beginning of your A level/BTEC courses how the component parts fit together.

This means knowing:

✓ what the component parts are
✓ how long you have to complete each unit or module

✓ what work you are expected to do
✓ how you'll be assessed

Courses are assessed in a variety of ways using a mix of coursework, assignments and exams. Be clear about which assignments and exams count towards your final assessment.

Find out how your work will be assessed and what criteria will be used. Get a copy of the specification and go through the section which relates to assessment.

Ask your teachers to explain the assessment criteria to you if you're unsure of anything.

Think long term

Sometimes we get so wrapped up in the issues of here-and-now that we forget to look further ahead.

Keeping a perspective on the long term means giving some consideration to the important events which lie ahead over each term, the year and over the course as a whole.

Find out when you have:
✓ exams or tests to sit
✓ assignments to complete
✓ fieldwork trips
✓ work experience to go on
✓ group projects to carry out
✓ presentations to make

Enter these key events into your study planner, as well as entering dates of holidays, UCAS deadlines, driving tests and other general reminders. Carry it around with you and get into the habit of updating it on a regular basis.

Plan ahead

Planning helps you to decide what you need to do now in order to get where you want to be in the future. You must be willing to give up some of your time and energy now in order to accomplish more later on.

Don't accept the myth that planning leads to less freedom and spontaneity. Time spent planning is not wasted time, it is time saved in the long run. It also minimises the stress that usually accompanies last minute assignment writing or revising for exams.

However, beware of over planning, which can serve as a way to put off getting down to real work.

Work consistently

Try to pace yourself by putting in a consistent amount of work each week, with extra impetus around key deadlines and exams.

As a general rule, each hour you spend in the classroom should be matched by at least one hour of independent study. This might include homework, coursework, background reading, revision, preparation for forthcoming lessons or meetings relating to group projects. Ask your teachers to clarify how many hours of work they expect you to do each week.

The beginning and end of each term are critical, so make sure you work during these times. Most students float through the first weeks of a course, believing that the hard work will come later.

Do more than the set work

Just doing the work set by your teachers may sound like the easy option, but doing a bit extra and reading around the subject has major benefits. Firstly, it helps to create interest which in turn increases motivation. Secondly, it enables you to get a much deeper and broader understanding of the subject. Base this extra work on what is in the course specification and set aside time each week to do it.

Review your work

Once you have finished a unit of work, or perhaps at the end of each half term, aim to 'revise' what you have covered.

Revision in this context means at the very least reading through and trying to understand the material covered in lessons. It could also mean condensing the material into some form of revision notes and is a time to copy up any work you've missed.

You will feel the benefit of adopting this approach when you need to revise for a test or exam as you will have already laid a good foundation of understanding.

Don't become a fanatic

Don't become a slave to time and to your personal time management system. Your time management tools can be good servants but can equally be bad masters. Using time effectively should always be your ideal but it should never become an obsession.

3

Getting Down To STUDY

Procrastination is the habit of putting things off and leads to tomorrow always being the busiest day of the week!

Make the most of study periods

Study periods are built into the timetable to enable you to focus in on the demands of the courses that you have chosen to study. It is so easy to fritter away these study periods playing games, watching videos or just chatting - especially during the early weeks of the new school year when study periods are a bit of a novelty!

Get into the habit of thinking ahead about what you might do in study periods. When you're packing your bag before you go to school, think not only of the items you need for the lessons you have but what you might also need so that you can work productively during your study periods. There is nothing more frustrating than thinking you will do some homework during a study period only to find out you haven't got the relevant notes or textbook with you.

Make it your aim to make full use of free periods as any time lost here will have to be made up from your own free time.

Get into a routine

The greatest difficulty for any student is simply getting down to regular work. In order to keep up with your workload you should aim to put aside certain hours for study and plan to do a regular amount of work each week.

You will make it much easier for yourself if your study schedule follows some sort of consistent routine. For instance, you might plan to study at a certain time each day, or study a particular subject during the same study period each week.

Go for excellence, not perfection

Perfectionists want everything just right before they can say a piece of work is finished. This can lead to endlessly polishing a task. Even worse, this often means that other more important tasks are put off because you keep adding unnecessary finishing touches.

Decide whether or not the extra effort you put in is worth it and ask yourself how close to perfect each piece of work has to be. Excellence is a good aim and is achievable. Perfection is neither achievable nor is it required by your teacher.

Try out the 10 minute rule

Sometimes, just getting started is the problem. If a task is really unpleasant just say to yourself you'll work on it for ten minutes and no more. This might be all you need to get the task underway.

Do an easy task first

If you have a large task to do, divide it into smaller more manageable steps. Make the very first step a small one and one which you will have no problem in doing.

Do the worst task early

If you find that you keep putting a task off day after day, make a decision to get it done first thing in the morning. If you get it out of the way early on in the day, you may even get a buzz from knowing you don't have it hanging over you anymore.

Countdown to work

Set the timer on your tablet or phone to count down from say 10 minutes and resolve to start work immediately it goes off.

Remind yourself

For really important tasks leave notes or sticky notes in your bedroom, on your folders or in your bag. Write the task on the note or sticky note and next to it in large letters write DO IT NOW!

Weigh things up

If you're really stuck and can't get started, think of the task in terms of weighing up the positives and negatives.

Positives may include:
- ✓ Peace of mind
- ✓ A sense of achievement
- ✓ Getting it out of the way

Negatives may include;
- ✗ Getting a low mark
- ✗ Sense of failure
- ✗ The nagging thought that the task has not been done

Usually, the positives far outweigh the negatives.

Get on with it!

We can all find a whole load of excuses why we can't get on with work –
just need to check my messages, too tired, wrong time of day, don't feel like
it, too hot, too cold and so on. If you wait for the ideal conditions you'll be
waiting for ever!

4

Getting More From
STUDY SESSIONS

*Two students work for one hour on an identical task. One student gets
more done than the other. Why is this? It's because some students
have discovered ways of getting more from their time!*

Beware interruptions and distractions

Distractions and interruptions cannot be eliminated completely, but they
can often be minimised.

Follow this 2-step approach:
Step 1: Identify which interruptions and distractions are a regular problem.
Step 2: Do something about them.

Try to be realistic and to work at reducing only those distractions
and interruptions that you can actually do something about. Here are
some examples:

Leave me alone!
When you are studying, give a signal to others that you are studying and
need to be left alone. This could mean simply telling your friends or family
politely, but firmly, that you would prefer not to be disturbed or even putting a note on the door. If necessary, use headphones or earplugs to cut out
external noise.

Find a hideaway
Sometimes studying where no-one knows where you are, such as in a library, is the only way to guarantee uninterrupted time. You can get twice as much done during uninterrupted time.

Put it away
If you surround yourself with things that might distract you, you are inviting yourself to be distracted.

For instance, if you have a magazine which you have just bought on the table in front of you it's only natural that you will be tempted to read it. If you're surrounded by books and folders from different subjects you may start thinking of another piece of work you need to do and lose your train of thought.

When you study, have in front of you only those things connected to the stuff that you are currently working on.

Digital distractions

Most people love to multi-task. Updating your status, liking photos, taking selfies, checking messages, emails and tweets and watching videos, whilst at the same time tackling a homework task, seems perfectly reasonable. However, whilst multi-tasking is great for some situations, it isn't for learning. Constantly switching your focus between an assignment and your phone inevitably results in you learning less and taking more time to get the work done.

Don't delude yourself into thinking that digital multi-tasking doesn't affect your learning, it is tiring for your brain and affects your ability to stay focused. Even if you are self-disciplined enough to limit the number of times you check your phone or tablet, a quick glance at a social networking site can end up in hours of browsing and video watching.

There is only one possible solution. Before you start studying, turn everything off (not just switched to silent!) and don't turn it on again until you've completely finished.

Even better than this, put your phone in another room. Now, that is a challenge!

When you do need to use your laptop, tablet or phone to carry out research on the internet resist the temptation to click on irrelevant video clips or links. Go full screen and close other tabs so they won't distract you.

Tackle one task at a time

It's all too easy to flit from one task to another when you have many different pieces of work to do. Doing this usually leads to getting very little done and then doing it poorly. Much time is wasted because you are continually picking up the threads of your thinking.

Uni-tasking is the key which means focusing on one task at a time and giving it your full attention. Stick with it until you finish it or you can't go any further, that way you will then feel that you have made some progress.

Set a target

When you sit down to study, think for a moment about what you are going to do during that study session. Don't just sit and aimlessly work without a target in mind. Your target might be to read a number of chapters in a text book, plan an essay or revise a topic. You could even make a quick note of your target.

Press on and finish

Some students have a tendency to stop working on a task just when they are in sight of completing it. When you are working on a task all the factors and issues are fresh in your mind. When you come back to it again you will have to spend time gathering your thoughts and ideas together before you can start again. Always press on and complete a task which you are close to finishing.

Plan your breaks

When you begin a study session, decide approximately how long you are going to study for. This could be for 30 minutes, one hour, two hours or longer. Make a note of the time when you start and decide roughly when you are going to take breaks during this time.

When you have a break, do something that creates a space between tasks and helps you to relax. This might include reading, going for a walk, exercise, listening to music, playing a musical instrument or even having a nap!

Reward yourself

If you work for a particular period of time or finish a task, what will be your reward? A reward is a strong motivator only if you use it after you achieve your goal, so don't give yourself the reward if you don't reach the goal! For rewards to work as motivators, select rewards that are worthwhile to you.

Rewards after study sessions might include checking your messages, watching a particular TV programme, gaming, phoning a friend, going out, eating a favourite snack or simply doing nothing.

End on a high note

Learn to end on a high note by trying to stop at a point of accomplishment. This could be finishing an essay plan, getting to the end of a chapter or completing a question.

Stopping mid-way through a task might play on your mind as it leaves you feeling that you've left something unfinished. It also means that when you return to the task you'll need to spend some time trying to remember the key ideas.

If you do stop doing some work which you will need to come back to, make sure you have a logical starting point when you return. You could leave a note reminding yourself of what the next task is or what difficulty caused you to stop working.

5

Improving your CONCENTRATION

All students have experienced that sinking feeling when concentration levels have reached rock-bottom and no work gets done. You can't magically improve your concentration but you can learn to manage it better!

Convince yourself of the benefits

The benefits of improving your concentration are numerous and can include:

> getting more done
> doing your best work
> saving time
> making fewer mistakes
> increased confidence in your ability
> peace of mind

Break and rest

Taking breaks is a great way of refreshing your powers of concentration. How long you study for before you take a break depends on you and the sort of work you are doing.

For routine work, breaks normally work best when taken every 20-40 minutes and last for about 5-10 minutes. However, some people can work for very long periods of time without needing to rest. Find out what works best for you.

Breaks don't necessarily have to involve leaving the room (where it is easy to get distracted) or stopping for long periods of time (when it is easy to make excuses not to get restarted).

Use your prime times wisely

Prime times are periods of the day when you feel at your most alert. Whenever possible, arrange to tackle difficult or complex tasks during your high-energy, peak alertness times of the day. If you do this regularly you will be able to work more quickly and to a higher standard.

One way of taking advantage of your prime times is to make a list of tasks which need doing and identify them as hard or easy. Use prime times for hard work and other times of the day for easy, interesting or routine work.

Write yourself reminders

When you are studying, all sorts of thoughts probably pop into your mind. These might include friends you need to message, arrangements to make, ideas you have, things you've forgotten to do and so on.

These thoughts can be very distracting and will normally take away your train of thought from the task you are working on. Even worse, they may stop you working altogether.

To lessen the negative effect this can have, get into the habit of keeping some sticky notes next to you so that you can write yourself a reminder about what's just popped into your head. You can then forget about it and get on with the task in hand.

Work actively

Passive studying can often lead to low levels of concentration. When you are studying, try to make sure you are doing something active such as taking notes, talking aloud, testing yourself or even getting up and walking around from time to time.

Avoid marathon sessions

Your concentration will suffer badly if you are forced to work for many hours at a time, as often occurs in situations where you've left everything until the last minute! These marathon sessions can be avoided by getting into the habit of doing a bit of studying every day.

Listen and learn?

Whether or not you listen to music whilst studying, is up to you. Only you can decide what helps and what distracts you.

Sometimes it is definitely beneficial to have no music at all. Such times might include when you are trying to memorise information, practising questions under exam conditions or trying to understand a difficult topic.

What is definitely disruptive to your learning is if you find yourself continually browsing through playlists to select individual songs to play whenever a track ends. So, if you do decide to put music on, press play and leave it!

One idea to try out is to play loud and energetic music during your breaks as a contrast to times when you are studying.

6

Getting more from YOUR DAY

Many students start the day with good intentions, but find at the end of the day that they didn't get round to doing half the things they set out to. But it doesn't have to be this way!

Use to-do lists

If there's one single habit which you should work hard to get into, it's writing a to-do list. A to-do list is simply a collection of the things you need to get done on a particular day.

It can be written on a notepad or using a to-do list app and is best done first thing in the morning, although some prefer to do it in the evening to cover the following day. You could write one every day or only on days when you've got a lot to get done.

Many students get great pleasure from ticking off the tasks they complete, either as they do them or at the end of the day. Some find it useful to write on their list the time of day to tackle specific tasks. Others include everything they have to do during a day, including those tasks not related to studying at all such as their part-time jobs, driving lessons, clubs, leisure interests, things to buy, people to contact etc etc.

First things first

Have you ever had the feeling at the end of a day that you didn't do the really important things or spent too little time on them? If so, then you are probably not sorting out your priorities. Here are two ways you can do this:

123 Method

A simple way of setting priorities is to number the tasks on your to-do list in order of importance 1, 2, 3 etc. Start working on no. 1 and stay with it until it's finished, or until you've done as much as you can, then start no. 2 and so on.

ABC Method

The ABC method simply means marking each task on your to-do list with an A, B, or C where:

A = a task you must do that day
B = a task you should do that day
C = a task you could do that day

Start working on your A tasks first and only go on to your B tasks if you finish your A tasks, then onto your C tasks if you finish your B tasks.

Estimate how long tasks will take

Having a good idea of how long something might take to do is very helpful when you're trying to fit everything into a busy day. However, most of us hugely underestimate how long tasks take.

For a task you are familiar with, estimate how long you think it will take to do and double it! For a task you are unfamiliar with, guess how long you think it will take and triple it!!

Build in slack time

It is important for your motivation that you don't finish every day with a list of tasks you haven't got round to doing. This is usually a sign that you are being too ambitious in what you set out to do.

As a rough guide, your to-do list should contain tasks that add up to about three quarters of the time you've set aside for studying. The extra quarter of your time that you've left open with nothing planned is known as slack time. This time should be used to deal with anything unexpected that turns up (it usually does!).

Use a master to-do list

A master to-do list can be used to keep a record of all the things you need to do both today and at sometime in the future, including big and small tasks, school related work and personal stuff. You can work from this on its own or use it alongside your daily to-do list.

It is useful because it can be used to write down the tasks which crop up during the day but which you are not going to tackle that day.

Be ready for down times

There are going to be times in the day when you won't be able to get on with your work. These could be times when you're waiting to see a teacher, are on the bus or the computer network crashes. These times are called 'down times'.

Prepare for down times by carrying around with you short and easy tasks which you can fit in during these odd moments.

7

Tackling Major
ASSIGNMENTS

*One of the most difficult tasks to tackle is one where a great deal
of work needs to be done over a long period of time.
Most of us leave these tasks until the last minute and then
have to suffer marathon late-night study sessions!*

Be clear about the task

One of the biggest time wasters is going ahead and doing lots of thinking
and information gathering without first having a clear idea of what you need
to do. Invest time at the beginning of an assignment focusing your thoughts
on the precise nature and scope of the task including the number of words,
how it needs to be presented, how it will be assessed and when it needs to
be finished by.

Set your own deadlines

An effective way to get yourself motivated to complete a piece of work on
time is to set yourself a challenging deadline for getting it finished.

Always make it your aim to finish the assignment before the deadline set
by your teacher. It's unlikely that you will finish earlier, but it will give you
some breathing space. Of course, starting early is the surest way there is for
getting something finished on time.

Sometimes you will have more than one assignment due in during the same week. These bunched deadlines can cause pressure points, where the demands on your time are greater than the time you have available. When this looks likely, bring one or more of the deadlines forward yourself.

Set mini-deadlines

If the deadline is some way off, set mini-deadlines that indicate when you should have reached a particular point in the assignment, for example, when you hope to finish the first draft.

Your mini-deadlines give you an opportunity to see how things are going. You can tell whether you are on track to meet your deadline, need to put in more time, adjust the next mini-deadline and so on.

Use a deadline diary

Put your deadlines and mini-deadlines in a diary/planner, on your phone, tablet, pc or wall planner as a reminder. In addition to school-related work, also include things such as dates for driving lessons and driving tests, UCAS deadlines and other major events.

Take small steps

Slice up the assignment into small 'bite-size' chunks or steps. Start by simply brainstorming all the steps which need to be taken before the whole assignment is finished. Then put the steps in order.

Most major assignments follow a series of predictable stages, for example:
> choosing and defining a topic
> researching, collecting and organising material
> preparing the first draft
> editing and polishing the final copy

When doing your planning, allow time for each of these stages and also allow time for thinking. For very large assignments you may find it useful to break down each step into specific tasks.

Get the pace right

Getting the pace right is about deciding when you're going to tackle individual tasks over a period of time. If, for example, you have six weeks in which to complete an assignment, ask yourself how many tasks you could tackle in the first week, then the second, and so on. It is particularly important to decide a starting date.

Organise resources

The resources you may need to tackle an assignment could range from books, internet, equipment or people you need to talk to. When planning an assignment decide what resources you will need, when you will need them, what their availability is and which you have to book or reserve in advance.

When gathering information from the internet, books and other sources, focus your search on the specific information you need. It's all too easy to copy out notes or print pages from such sources only to find that most of it isn't needed. Make a note of where you found all the material in case you need to go back to it.

Allow slack time

Building slack into your deadline means allowing more time than you think necessary when setting deadlines. This slack time can prove invaluable if a task takes much longer than you think, or an additional task is given to you without any notice, or you're ill for a few days or your laptop plays up (as they usually do at the worst possible moment!).

Start with something quick and easy

It's easy to put off starting a major assignment when you know it will involve many hours of concentrated work. To get yourself started, make the first task a quick and simple one and one that won't take too much effort or time to get done.

8

Organising Your WORKSPACE

At first glance, ideas for organising workspace may seem only to save a few seconds of time. But when added together, these precious seconds soon add up!

Get the environment right

If properly set up, your environment can be a valuable tool and can directly affect your ability to concentrate. If you work in your own room surround yourself with things that remind you of past successes and happy moments, such as photos, medals and certificates.

Some like a structured working environment – desk, chair, orderly work area. Others unstructured – kitchen table, easy chair, everything out in front of them. Some find a mixture of the two works best.

Lighting is also important, so make sure your work area is getting sufficient light, particularly natural light if possible.

Tidy up between tasks

Get into the habit of tidying your workspace between tasks and at the end of any study session.

Tidying up your desk after you've finished something means that when you next sit down it is clear and more welcoming. It also means that you can decide what to do next without being influenced by what is in front of you.

Have a clear filing system

A clear filing system has to meet the following definition: the ability to find what you want, when you want it. It is not necessarily orderly and neat, but it does need to make sense.

Create your own system and then put it to a 2-minute-test: can you find any folder, book or piece of paper in less than two minutes?

From time to time your filing system will probably end up resembling a rubbish tip. This is not a good reason to dismiss the need for a filing system, it simply means that you need to give it an overhaul. This might involve simply putting everything back where it belongs or changing it to make it work better. Filing systems may need overhauling at the end of a unit, topic, term or year. It's amazing how clearing your filing system clears the mind!

Avoid dumping grounds

Avoid dumping grounds for folders and books, such as chairs and the floor. This will only lead to piles of paperwork where it can prove difficult to quickly find what you're looking for. If you haven't got enough room for your folders and books, get some shelves put up.

Keep things in one place

Keeping your folders in one place rather than scattered all round your room or house means you can find them more easily. Those people who claim to know where everything is when their folders are thrown everywhere are usually just kidding themselves. Store those folders you use most often in the most easily accessible places.

Make sure folders are clearly labelled

Here are a few ideas:

✓ label folders on the outside
✓ use dividers inside
✓ make an index in the front of each folder
✓ write page numbers on your notes
✓ put loose sheets of paper in punched plastic pockets
✓ keep labels up to date

Labelling folders is stating the obvious, but it's worth repeating as poorly labelled folders are the source of much wasted time.

The same attention should be paid when managing your computer files. Take care when naming, labelling and storing files, making sure they are appropriately named and easy to locate.

Making The Most Of REVISION TIME

There is no escaping the fact that revision involves long hours and sometimes boring work.

Get set

The very first day of your revision should be spent organising and planning:

✓ get a copy of the specification and bookmark the exam board website
✓ make sure you've got a full set of course notes and that they are properly filed
✓ buy filecards, pens, highlighters etc.
✓ buy revision guides and identify useful revision websites and videos

List the topics

Your first bit of planning involves simply making a list of the topics and subtopics you have covered. Use your notes or the course specification for this but if you're not sure ask your teacher.

Find the gaps

It is important to establish which topics you are confident in and which you are weak at. One way to find the gaps in your understanding is to work through some past papers, making a note as you go along of the topics you find difficult. Mock papers you have sat previously will also give clues to your strengths and weaknesses.

Plot your route

Once you have made a list of topics to cover and know your strengths and weaknesses, decide the order to tackle them in. You don't need to go through the specification from start to finish and you don't have to revise topics in the order you were taught them - work out your own route.

One suggestion is to make your very first revision topic an easy one as this will build your confidence. Then move on to some difficult topics before going back to some easier ones to finish with.

Break up the day

A manageable way to break up the day is to do it in blocks. You can divide the day into 1-hour or 2-hour blocks or simply morning, afternoon and evening. Decide how many blocks to revise on a daily or weekly basis.

Have a plan

Revising when you feel like it or for the odd hour here and there is not going to be enough. Writing a realistic daily or weekly revision timetable allows you to cover all the topics you need to but remember to mix up your strong/weak, interesting/boring subjects. If you don't like timetables, simply make a list of the revision tasks you want to achieve at the beginning of each day.

Three more ideas!

Here are a few suggestions for you to consider:
- ✓ Work hard early on in the day as this gives you a good (and guilt free!) feeling for the rest of the day.
- ✓ Build in some time immediately before the exam period starts for tackling whole exam papers under timed exam conditions.
- ✓ Be good to yourself - leave one day a week when you do not revise.

10

Going For The TOP GRADES

> *High achieving students achieve their success by developing and consistently applying effective study habits. But it's not just a case of working smarter, it's about working harder too!*

Go the extra mile

If you want to achieve the top A level grades you'll have to do more than just the work set by your teachers. Do extra reading and research into the subjects you are studying, based around what's in the course specification. Start doing this extra studying from the very beginning of Year 12 and sustain it right through to your final exams.

Print off a copy of the specification for each subject (or maybe just the unit you are studying at the time), put it in the front of your folder for that subject and use it to keep a track of the topics you are covering. Your teachers probably won't have time to cover every line of the whole specification, so identify any areas that don't get covered and then make it your job to fill in these gaps.

Understand as you go

With the extra depth and quantity of study required in the Sixth Form, it is important to understand things as you go along rather than leaving it until you have to revise for a test or exam.

To make sure you do understand what you are being taught, put aside a few minutes every day to review the notes you took in your lessons that day or, when that's not possible, within 24 hours. Check your understanding, fill in information gaps and identify any questions you have for your teacher – as soon as possible after the lesson when it's still fresh in your mind.

Revise from day one

With so much to learn and remember, revision isn't something you can afford to leave until the period immediately before the final exams. Whether it's writing revision cards or tackling extra questions, watching videos or reading textbooks, revision is something you should be doing from the very beginning.

You'll really feel the benefit of having done some on-going revision when you start your final revision push. It should help prevent you from feeling overwhelmed by the amount you've got to learn.

Make full use of your teachers

Your teachers are probably the best study resource you have. Get to know them well as they're experts and can provide important insights into their subject.

In the first week or two of the September term make a special point of going to see each of your teachers outside of normal lesson times - most will be delighted to see you and to answer any questions you may have. Then make going to see them a regular thing.

When teachers hand you back work, or you sit a test, make sure you're clear about any written comments they've made and ask them what you can do to improve your work.

When you receive termly or annual progress reports ask your teachers to clarify and expand on target grades, predicted grades and any other comments.

Get the most out of lessons

You spend many hours in lessons every week and this is priceless learning time - so you can't afford to waste any of it. Always ask questions and participate so that you are fully engaged in the lesson, even if you think you understand everything.

To help you to follow lessons and to participate more fully, try reading ahead of the topic you are covering in class. Doing this on a regular basis will give you a much better chance of understanding what you are taught first time around – a major benefit. Ask your teacher which topics are being covered for the next few weeks and tell them why you want to know.

Note-taking in class can be a very passive activity, so when copying notes from the whiteboard or working through a handout always add your own comments as this makes you think and helps learning.

Take care where you study

The environment you study in, whether at home or in school, has a major impact on how effectively you study. Wherever you study make sure there is nothing to distract you, whether it be friends, your phone (turn it off), siblings, your phone (don't have it next to you), background noise or your phone (put it in a different room!).

It is particularly important that you make the most of study periods, so find a place to spend them where you won't be distracted or interrupted (leave your phone in your bag!).

Make the most of exam board websites

Exam board websites are packed full of useful information, so bookmark them. Make full use of the course specification, past papers, specimen papers, mark schemes, examiners' reports and information on UMS/grade boundaries.

Do as many past papers as possible, maybe more than once, and keep a record of all the exam papers you have tried (the year and the unit) and the mark/grade you got. To make the most of past papers look carefully at the mark schemes to see what things you actually get marks for and take note of any key words, phrases or ideas that are mentioned.

Maintain your motivation

Staying motivated is a key issue for all Sixth Form students, so give some serious thought at the beginning of Year 12 to your reasons for studying. What grades do you want to achieve for each of the subjects you are studying? Are you hoping to follow a particular career? Do you have a university or degree course in mind?

Put some time and effort into researching potential career pathways, looking at university prospectuses and finding out about the entrance requirements for possible degree courses. When you do feel demotivated, which you undoubtedly will at times, think about these future plans.

Get the balance right

Studying in the Sixth Form inevitably involves a great deal of hard work. But a healthy work-life balance should allow time for other pursuits, hobbies and social activities. If at any time you are having difficulty with balancing the demands of school work with life outside of the Sixth Form go and talk to your Tutor or Head of Sixth Form about it.

Hope that's been useful.

I wish you every SUCCESS!

GO FOR IT!!!